BLACKSMITH SHOPS OF ZIKLAG

PUBLISHING

copyright, Dr Don Lynch, 2016

All international rights reserved.

ISBN-13: 978-1540500168

ISBN-10: 1540500160

For more information:

MinistryMatrix
www.freedomhouse.rocks

BLACKSMITH SHOPS OF ZIKLAG

DR DON LYNCH

PUBLISHING

BLACKSMITH SHOPS OF ZIKLAG

"I have created the blacksmith who fans the coals beneath the forge and makes the weapons of destruction. And I have created the armies that destroy." (Isaiah 54:16)

"The following men joined David at Ziklag while he was hiding from Saul son of Kish. They were among the warriors who fought beside David in battle.

All of them were expert archers, and they could shoot arrows or sling stones with their left hand as well as their right. They were all relatives of Saul from the tribe of Benjamin.

Some brave and experienced warriors from the tribe of Gad also defected to David while he was at the stronghold in the wilderness. They were expert with both shield and spear, as fierce as lions and as swift as deer on the mountains." (1 Chronicles 12:1)

ZIKLAG LEADERSHIP TEST

The last great test of David's leadership comes at Ziklag. He has moved through leadership maturity from shepherd to worshipper, to warrior, to general, to ruler, and he is standing at the brink of his leadership. His army is strong, trained, well supplied – for a reason we shall soon discuss – and he is about to face his greatest challenge as a kingdom leader.

But first, let's examine why David rules Ziklag, the city of Israel's enemy, and how this prophesies to Brasil in this season of her spiritual development. Spiritual development comes before cultural development. All the conditions we can observe in the natural come as result of conditions we must discern in the spirit. Since we are the ones representing God in establishing and expanding spiritual conditions that will produce natural conditions, the change that need to be made must be made in, by, and through us.

David receives greater preparation and experience as the ruler of Ziklag before he rules Israel. In that way, David leads at the level of leadership God's purpose requires.

> 1. We can be ready for leadership at many levels without being ready for leadership at the level that fulfills God's purpose, for us personally and the kingdom corporately.
>
> 2. We can be faithful at every level of our preparation yet require additional intense testing to step up to the next level.
>
> 3. We can only measure our leadership by what we can sustain, not what we can obtain or do occasionally.

Remember, Jesus faced His greatest tests at the end, and "though He was a Son, yet learned His obedience by the things He passionately endured and became completely and mature. In this way, becoming the Source of eternal rescue to all those that obey Him."

Jesus experienced the Gethsemane oil

Blacksmith Shops of Ziklag

press, the crush of the whip, the hammer of shattering betrayal, and burning fires of forging that made Him the Father's weapon of destruction: "He destroyed the works of the devil! He endured passionately and became complete and mature in His leadership and purpose.

Ziklag is the city David received from the enemy during his exile from his place of destiny.

    1. Do not think that God's purpose is out of reach just because you are ruling Ziklag instead of ruling Israel.

    2. Do not think your enemy is King Saul and the failed regime of insufficient obedience.

    3. Do not think that ruling Ziklag is your final destiny or destination.

David is not in Ziklag because of failure anymore than Jesus was in Gethsemane because of failure. David came to Ziklag because of faithfulness as Jesus came to Gethsemane because of His faithfulness.

David is not in Ziklag to wait for the day of his purpose. David is not in Ziklag to mourn or complain. David is in Ziklag to prepare his leadership, his army, and to restore a specific aspect of infrastructure for the kingdom.

Blacksmith Shops of Ziklag

THE PREVAILING SPIRITUAL CONDITION

Remember the condition of Israel when David killed Goliath? Remember the word I released to Brasil, for example, two years ago, that God was giving Brasil new weapons for a new season? That is also true of America! Remember that when David arrived at the battle, no warrior in Israel had a sword or weapon because the Philistines had shut down all the blacksmith shops in Israel?

A whole generation grew up without weapons; and, no blacksmiths were in training, because no blacksmith shops existed in the nation.

David killed the giant. The army chased the Philistines and took their weapons. David put a weapon in the hand of every warrior in Israel in one day! Now, David is in exile, living on land controlled by the enemy.

But, Ziklag is strategic!

The name, "Ziklag" is composed of two ancient Hebrew words that mean "to pour" and "to press." Combined they describe the process of smelting iron, forging it into weapons, and pressing it into shape. In other words, Ziklag is a blacksmith center!

David has his own weapons factory in Ziklag, breaking the enemy's exclusive control on blacksmiths, allowing David's army to

Blacksmith Shops of Ziklag

train blacksmiths, design and build, even field test new weapons. David restores the glaring empty place in the kingdom infrastructure that has put Israel in a position of weakness with her enemies for decades.

While living in exile, running from Saul, God positions David in Ziklag so he can become the strongest king in the nation's history! David becomes a supplier of the very thing the enemy sought to limit! David comes into kingship with the missing piece of kingdom establishing and expansion so the kingdom is no longer on the defense.

Ziklag is strategic for David. He will come to the throne with his own army, wealth, and the key that will restore the infrastructure of the kingdom.

[The Philistines jealously guarded their monopoly on metal forging and blacksmithing. Hebrews were forced to pay them even for sharpening their agricultural implements. (1Sam.13.21). This situation has been confirmed by archaeology; the Philistines were in the Iron Age when they came to Palestine; the Hebrews attained to this level of advance only in the time of David.]

We need to forge kingdom weapons! We need to restore what the enemy has taken so we can rebuild kingdom infrastructure. Without it, we are left to fight with harvesting tools. Without it the harvesting tools remain dull because we need a blacksmith to sharpen them.

This is the season of the blacksmith shops!

We need to move from watching David wield the giant's sword to having a sword of our own. Then, we need to move from possessing available swords we find to blacksmith production of weapons that fit each warrior personally. Additionally, we need to move into blacksmith production of warriors so we can forge the hearts of warriors, pressed and poured into the heated molds, hammered while red with passion, formed into elite weapons. We must forge both weapons and warriors to wield them, making weapons that fit the hands of trained elite troops.

1. Blacksmiths do finishing work.

I want to challenge leaders to reach for finishing work, to bring leaders higher in preparation for the next level of kingdom expansion. Polishing isn't as important as finishing. Blacksmiths sharpen the blades and points, repair cracks or temper softened steel. They continue to make improvements on existing weapons, even designing and building new weapons with new designs.

It is certain that maturing our

Blacksmith Shops of Ziklag

leaders will require new weapon design and manufacturing. They will start imagining ways to improve that will challenge blacksmiths. Ziklag provides us with this capacity and capability.

The enemy wants us without weapons, so he empties the land of blacksmiths. When a greater season for kingdom establishing comes, we restore the blacksmiths to the land so they can design and build new weapons for a new generation of warriors.

2. We need to forge leaders to design, test, and use these weapons.

Our leadership training must step up if we are to be ready for this new opportunity to establish kingdom. We cannot accumulate believers as our measurement of success and ignore the development of champions needed to function at a higher level. We need training schools of warfare that recognize leaders who have purpose and potential at the regional, national, and international levels. And, we need blacksmith shops where these champions can receive both the new weapons and the training they need to use the

Blacksmith Shops of Ziklag

new weapons they imagine.

Remember the words of Hebrews 5:12: "For though by this time you ought to be teachers, you have need again for someone to teach you the elementary principles."

The training new leaders need to design, test, and use new weapons is as much wind, fire, and hammer as it is about the steel of which these weapons are made. We need to apply the blacksmith shop processes to our leaders! They need to experience the shattering of raw material, the fires that melt and separate the impurities, then feel the hammer upon the red steel, again and again, sparks flying into the air, to be plunged into the water for tempering.

3. We need spiritual blacksmiths to forge the endurance, strength, character, and tensile strength of champions!

David killed Goliath because of his character. As he matured, the sword of Goliath would have required sharpening, and Ziklag was the place where he improved the quality of his sword. David made Goliath's sword a better weapon as he matured as a general, ruler, and king!

In the next five years, schools that produce a new level of leadership must be restored to the kingdom infrastructure. These schools take the existing remnant to another level of endurance, skill, boldness, and wisdom. These schools measure the tensile strength of character, and examine the blade for fatal flaws.

We cannot produce the leaders needed to take the land without producing the leaders who can possess the land. The warriors that take the land must be led by warfare leaders who can possess the land.

It is not what a person can do as much as what he or she can sustain that marks the kingdom leadership level we require now.

Blacksmith Shops of Ziklag

THREE WAVES OF WARRING LEADERS

I see us preparing and sending three waves of warring leaders into battle in the next five years. The first wave rushes straight forward as strategic invaders of strategic positions, engaging the enemy in hand-to-hand combat. That wave will awaken the enemy's archers.

The second wave will face the enemy's arrows flying over the first wave. Oneness will be absolutely essential to this wave because we must lock shields to ward off the landing arrows while still moving forward under in this rainstorm of arrows. We will meet the enemy face to face if we move in oneness, and the enemy will be devastated at the front lines by this victory!

The third wave comes immediately behind the second with spears to push the enemy back at the points the enemy has been weakened by the first two waves.

So, the primary weapons of these three waves are;

> 1) the sword of the Spirit, the strategic rhema of God, and the battle plan calls for superior weapons of revelation;
>
> 2) the shield of faith and breast-

plate of righteousness provides superior defense against the enemy's existing arrow technology;

3) the spear, because the enemy will be moving backward to avoid confrontation, and the spear will counter this positioning and keep the enemy off balance while the first and second waves continue to tear holes in the frontlines and push into the interior ranks, the very heart, of the opposition.

WEAPONS OF AWAKENING

Paul also contrasts the weapons of light or daytime with the weapons of nighttime or sleeping: he is discussing the kind of weapons we should carry when Awakening comes to a region or nation.

"Recognizing the season, you can discern that already it is time for you to awake out of sleep: for now, rescue is nearer to us than when we first believed. The night is far spent, and the day is at hand: let us therefore throw off what we did when it was dark, and let us put on the armor of light. Let us live appropriate to daylight." (Romans 13:11-13)

A fresh wind of revival is blowing over the

kingdom that will be stronger than the wind that blew at any other time. This wind will have the potential to move revival into Awakening. The weapons of the day will be the new weapons forged by the blacksmith shops in anticipation of this daytime warfare.

Paul says, "Once the day fully arrives, you need to use the weapons of light."

We cannot prepare leaders for this Awakening once it begins unless we have blacksmith shops in place. We must prepare leaders now who have skill and expertise with the weapons of the daytime. We must prepare them now.

Leaders and blacksmiths who accurately anticipate what is coming next and prepare the Lord a people ready to respond in the new season!

WARRIORS PRESSED, POURED, AND POUNDED INTO SHAPE

The same principles that forge weapons also forge the warriors that wield those weapons. The iron ore is shattered to dust by heavy blows, then melted by the fires of purification and cleaning, before being poured into the molds of renewed minds, to be pounded by the shocks of the sledges and pressed by the olive

Blacksmith Shops of Ziklag

press of Gethsemane more deeply into personal layers of strength and endurance.

Ziklag tests your soul. You must become the warrior who can wield the new weapons when the blacksmith shops return to the kingdom. This process of preparation must be intense, and we cannot spare champions this process of pressing, pounding, pouring, and purification! We do not need pretty boys and girls but determined and courageous men and women with a fierceness of soul.

Now, in this generation are men and women called and prepared to establish blacksmith shops. Without larger numbers and elaborate structures, light the fires and set the anvils. This is blacksmith's work. You won't be training everybody, but you will be forging the character of champions and spiritual weapons!

In every region, blacksmith shops should be fully functional, and seasoned warriors wielding new weapons must be positioned as we move into 2017. The infrastructure of blacksmiths should be restored to the kingdom by 2020! Do not be afraid to create elite schools that train only the serious and committed. Continue with the present discipling training available to all, but provide something for elite troops when you identify prospects for championship level leaders.

Many people in this generation are called to preparation that requires blacksmiths, and

Blacksmith Shops of Ziklag

some are called to become blacksmiths themselves. These are the champions who will become the new warriors who design, test, and use new weapons, but they will also lead with a fathering heart. They will not fear the fire in themselves or the same burning in those they train. They endure the training and tests required for this army of David's, as nations come into the season of Awakening Revival.

TAKE ACTION NOW!

Let's return to our opening Scripture:
"The following men joined David at Ziklag. They joined the warriors who fought beside David in battle."

To be in this army, you need to join David at Ziklag! You need to go down to the blacksmith shop. You need to find and align with men and women of this caliber of leadership.

Ziklag is the place of pressing and pouring, the place of brokenness and reshaping. The place of finishing work that turns raw materials into God's weapons of advancement.

You need to feel the shocks that shatter the raw material, the wind that blows the fire to white hot heat, the forging coals that consume impurities and soften the soul for the hammer, so the process shapes you into God's weapon for this season of Awakening Revival!

Will you answer this call?

Blacksmith Shops of Ziklag

1. We must restore the infrastructure of the kingdom; we must restore the blacksmith shops!

2. We must establish the blacksmith shops of Ziklag in every region! The places of pressing and pouring must be built and become functional! Ziklags not only have blacksmiths, they produce blacksmiths.

3. We must design, forge, and test new weapons that will present us with a new level of warfare, a new level of leadership, and a new strategy for taking the land so we can possess the land.

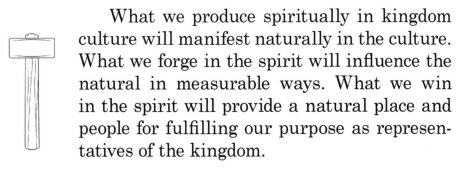

What we produce spiritually in kingdom culture will manifest naturally in the culture. What we forge in the spirit will influence the natural in measurable ways. What we win in the spirit will provide a natural place and people for fulfilling our purpose as representatives of the kingdom.

For more information on Dr Don Lynch Ministries, FreedomHouse, MinistryMatrix, and other outstanding teaching and training materials by Dr Don go to our website:

www.freedomhouse.rocks

Made in the USA
Middletown, DE
01 January 2021